# The Science of a Bicycle

## The Science of Forces

## By Ian Graham

Science and Curriculum Consultant:
Debra Voege, M.A., *Science Curriculum Resource Teacher*

**Gareth Stevens**
Publishing

Please visit our web site at **www.garethstevens.com**.
For a free color catalog describing Gareth Stevens Publishing's list of high-quality books,
call 1-800-542-2595 (USA) or 1-800-387-3178 (Canada). Gareth Stevens Publishing's fax: 1-877-542-2596

**Library of Congress Cataloging-in-Publication Data**
Graham, Ian, 1953–
    The science of a bicycle : the science of forces / by Ian Graham.
      p. cm. — (The science of ?)
    Includes bibliographical references and index.
    ISBN-10: 1-4339-0040-8    ISBN-13: 978-1-4339-0040-2 (lib. bdg. : alk. paper)
    1. Force and energy—Experiments—Juvenile literature. 2. Science—Experiments—
Juvenile literature. 3. Bicycles—Experiments—Juvenile literature. I. Title.
    QC73.4.G69   2008
    531'.6078—dc22                           2008034029

This North American edition first published in 2009 by
**Gareth Stevens Publishing**
A Weekly Reader® Company
1 Reader's Digest Road
Pleasantville, NY 10570-7000 USA

This U.S. edition copyright © 2009 by Gareth Stevens, Inc.
Original edition copyright © 2008 by Franklin Watts. First published in Great Britain
in 2008 by Franklin Watts, 338 Euston Road, London NW1 3BH, United Kingdom.

For Discovery Books Limited:
Editor: Rebecca Hunter              Designer: Keith Williams
Illustrator: Stefan Chabluk         Photo researcher: Rachel Tisdale

Gareth Stevens Executive Managing Editor: Lisa M. Herrington
Gareth Stevens Senior Editor: Barbara Bakowski
Gareth Stevens Creative Director: Lisa Donovan
Gareth Stevens Electronic Production Manager: Paul Bodley
Gareth Stevens Cover Designer: Keith Plechaty
Gareth Stevens Publisher: Keith Garton
Special thanks to Laura Anastasia, Michelle Castro, and Jennifer Ryder-Talbot

**Photo credits:** Shutterstock, cover; Getty Images/Hulton Archive, p. 4; Getty Images/Paul Chesley, p. 5;
istockphoto.com/VikaValter, p. 6; istockphoto.com/Michael Smith, p. 7; istockphoto.com/Oleg Kozlov, p. 8;
Rebecca Hunter, p. 9; Getty Images/Ariel Skelley, p. 10; Getty Images/John Nordell/The Christian Science Monitor,
p. 11; Discovery Picture Library, p. 12; istockphoto.com/Silvia Jansen, p. 13 top; Getty Images/Doug Pensinger, p.
13 bottom; istockphoto.com/Mario Savoia, p. 15; Getty Images/Barry Durrant, p. 16; istockphoto.com/Martin
Krammer, p. 17 top; Rebecca Hunter, p. 17 bottom; istockphoto.com/Maxim Petrichuk, p. 19; Discovery Picture
Library, p. 20; Discovery Picture Library, p. 21; istockphoto.com/Kledge, p. 22; istockphoto.com/James Ferrie,
p. 23 top; istockphoto.com/Shariff Che'lah, p. 23 bottom; Rebecca Hunter, p. 24; CFW Images/Chris Fairclough,
p. 25; istockphoto.com/Andrew Howe, p. 27 top; Getty Images/Javier Soriano, p. 28; Corbis/Olivier
Labalette/TempSport, p. 29 top; Corbis/Duomo, p. 29 bottom. Every effort has been made to trace copyright
holders. We apologize for any inadvertent omissions and would be pleased to insert appropriate
acknowledgments in a subsequent edition.

Printed in the United States of America
1 2 3 4 5 6 7 8 9 10 09 08

# Contents

Words that appear in **boldface** type are in the glossary on page 30.

# Bi-y-l B i-

There is a lot of science at work when you ride a bike. Staying upright, pedaling, steering, and turning require a careful balancing act. You do all that without even thinking about it!

## Taking Shape

Bicycles have a long history. The first two-wheelers were made in the early 1800s. Since then the bike has continued to grow more popular. About 100 million bicycles are made worldwide each year.

Bicycles didn't always look as they do today. Designers have tried out many different shapes. One of the most unusual bikes was the penny-farthing, or high-wheeler. The rider sat perched on top of a huge front wheel with pedals at its center. The bicycle had a tiny wheel at the back.

Penny-farthings were fast, but they had faults. Getting on them was hard! A bump or a sudden stop could tip a rider over the handlebars, too. Eventually, bike designers found that a diamond-shaped frame with two equal-size wheels worked best.

*◀ The penny-farthing had a giant front wheel. The rider had to climb on and start pedaling before the bike fell over!*

► In parts of China, India, and some other countries, there are few cars. Many people use bicycles and tricycles to get around.

## Built for Strength

If you look closely at a bike frame, you will see that it is made up of two triangles back to back. A bicycle frame made of triangles can support more than 10 times its own **weight**.

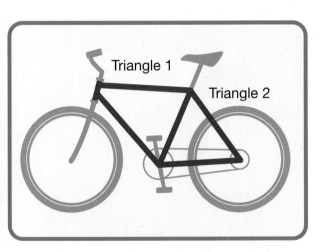

The triangle is a strong shape. It cannot be twisted out of shape without changing the length of one of its sides or breaking one of the joints between its sides. Builders use triangles to make structures strong. The famous Eiffel Tower in Paris, France, is made up of many triangles.

## Metal or Plastic?

The first bikes were made of wood or iron. Today, most bikes are made of steel or aluminum. Steel can stand up to the knocks and bumps of everyday riding. Makers often use aluminum instead, because it is lighter. Titanium bikes are even lighter and stronger than those made of aluminum. Titanium is very expensive and harder to shape, though. Some bikes are made of **carbon fiber**, a type of plastic material that is lighter and stronger than steel.

### Welding

The parts of a steel bike are joined together by welding. Steel is welded by heating the parts until they melt where they touch. The liquid metal from the two parts runs together and hardens as it cools, forming a strong joint.

5

**Forces** are pushes and pulls. They make objects **accelerate**, or change their speed or direction. Forces make bikes go faster, slow down, turn corners, and sometimes fall over. Some of the forces that act on bicycles are forces of nature. Others are forces made by a bike's rider.

## Balancing Forces

When a bike is not moving, two forces act on it. **Gravity** pulls the bike downward. The ground pushes back with an upward force against the bike. The two forces are perfectly in balance.

### Newton's Laws of Motion

Objects obey three **laws of motion** discovered by English scientist Sir Isaac Newton (1642–1727).

1. An object stays still or goes in a straight line at a steady speed unless a force acts on it.
2. When a force acts on an object, the object accelerates in the direction of the force.
3. To every action (force) there is an equal and opposite reaction (another force).

▲ A motionless bike demonstrates the first and third of Newton's laws of motion. No force pushes the bike forward, so it doesn't accelerate (first law). The downward pull of gravity on the bike is balanced by an equal and opposite force from the ground (third law).

▲ *A bicycle speeds up as it goes downhill. The force of gravity pulling the bike down the slope makes it accelerate (Newton's second law of motion).*

# Something in the Air

When you ride a bike, two more forces are in action. The first force is made by your feet pushing the pedals to make the bike move forward. The second force is made by the air around you. When an object moves through air, it pushes the air out of its way. The air pushes back. The pushing force of the air is called **air resistance**, or drag. If the pedaling force is greater than the drag, the bike goes faster. If drag is greater, the bike slows down. You must push the pedals harder to cycle into a strong wind. There is more air resistance to overcome.

# Gravity at Work

When you ride a bike on level ground, gravity does not affect your speed. When you cycle downhill, however, the pull of gravity makes you go faster. When you cycle uphill, gravity acts like a brake, slowing you down. That's why it's such hard work to cycle up a steep hill!

Machines, engines, and vehicles of all kinds are affected by a force called **friction**. Friction resists the sliding of objects against each other. Some parts of a bike work because of friction. Others work better without it.

## What Is Friction?

If you could look at the smooth surface of an object through a high-power microscope, it would look like a mountain range with peaks and valleys. Even a surface that appears to be perfectly smooth has rough areas.

When two pieces of metal slide against each other, the high peaks in the surfaces hit each other and make it harder for the pieces to slide. Rougher surfaces catch against each other even more, causing greater friction. Friction between the moving parts of a bike acts like a brake, slowing the bike down. Friction acts in the opposite direction to the bike's movement.

▶ *The nuts and bolts that hold a bike together stay tight because of friction.*

8

# Good Friction

Some parts of a bike rely on friction. They would not work without it. Friction between the tires and the ground lets the tires push against the ground and move a bike. Without friction, the wheels would spin, but the bike wouldn't move. Friction makes the brakes work. It keeps your feet from sliding off the pedals. Friction lets you grip the handlebars tightly, too.

▲ Oil reduces friction between a bike's moving parts so they can slide more easily.

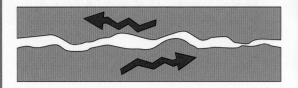

▲ *Friction happens because the rough parts of surfaces hit each other while trying to slide past each other.*

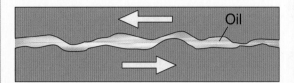

▲ *The addition of oil reduces friction, making the surfaces slide over each other more easily.*

# Bad Friction

Some parts of a bike have to slide against each other. The pedals and wheels have to turn easily. These moving parts are oiled to make them more slippery. The chain needs to slide on and off **teeth** on the **gearwheels**. Bicycle oil coats the surfaces of moving parts so that they don't catch against each other as much. Without oil, these parts would rub against each other more, slowing the bike. The parts would wear out faster, too.

# A Balancing Act

The famous scientist Albert Einstein (1879–1955) said, "Life is like riding a bicycle. To keep your balance, you must keep moving." A rider must constantly make small changes in position and steering to stay upright.

## Tipping Point

Every object has a base of support. It also has a point called its **center of gravity**. An object stays balanced if its center of gravity is over its base. If the object leans so that its center of gravity moves outside its base, the object tips over.

▲ *Training wheels can be attached to the back of a bicycle to create a wide base. A bike with training wheels does not tip over easily.*

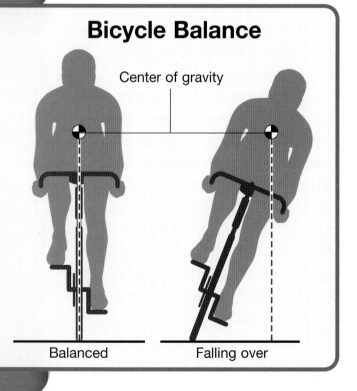

### Bicycle Balance

Center of gravity

Balanced    Falling over

An object with a wide base and a low center of gravity is stable, or hard to push over. For example, a pyramid is stable. Objects with a small base and a high center of gravity are unstable. They fall over more easily. A pencil standing on end is unstable. Give it one tiny push and it falls over!

## On Base

When you ride a bike, most of your weight is at the top of the bike, so your center of gravity is high. Your base is very small—just the width of the tires on the ground. You're a bit like a pencil standing on end. You need to keep turning the handlebars slightly to stay balanced. If the bike starts to fall to one side, you need to steer in that direction to keep your center of gravity above your base.

## Spinning Wheels

If you give your bike a push and set it moving forward, it doesn't fall over immediately. How can such an unstable object balance by itself?

The bicycle's wheels behave like **gyroscopes**. A gyroscope is a spinning wheel that tries to keep going in the same direction, like a spinning top. When a bike with no rider starts to lean to one side, its front wheel automatically turns in the same direction and stops the bicycle from falling over. When the bike slows down, the self-steering effects grow weaker. Eventually, the bicycle falls over, just as a spinning top does when it slows down.

**11**

# Steer Clear

There is more to steering a bike than just turning the handlebars. Steering involves a tricky balancing act that seems to defy gravity. When you steer a bike around a turn, you must balance forces that keep changing size and direction.

## It's Your Turn

Imagine you are riding your bike in a straight line. You want to turn right. What do you do? Do you simply turn the handlebars to the right? Oops! If you do that, you'll fall over!

When an object moves, it tries to keep going in the same direction. If you turn your bike's handlebars to the right, the bicycle turns right—but your body tries to keep moving straight ahead! The bike topples over to its left.

## Leaning to Balance

Leaning into a turn keeps a bike balanced. How do you make a bike lean? You can shift your weight to one side and let gravity pull the bike over. Another way is to turn the handlebars the wrong way. It may sound strange, but you can make a bike lean to the right by briefly turning the handlebars to the left! That action is called **countersteering**. The

◀ *A bike must lean in order to turn. An upright bike can only go straight.*

▲ *It's all in the lean! To make a bike turn, the rider has to make it lean into the turn at exactly the right angle.*

bike is thrown off balance and starts to topple. Before it falls, turning the handlebars back to the right makes it turn smoothly.

## Rubber on the Road

The amount you have to lean when turning a bike depends on your speed and the sharpness of the turn. The faster you go and the tighter the turn, the more you must lean. But watch out! If you lean too far, the tires may lose their grip on the ground, and the bike may slide out from under you!

### Slip Sliding Away

When a bike leans in a turn, friction between the tires and the ground keeps the bike from sliding sideways. There is less friction when the ground is slippery. Take extra care when riding on slippery ground.

▼ *Friction stops a bike from falling during a turn, unless the rider leans over too far or the ground is slippery.*

# Pedal Power

Bicycle wheels turn when you push the pedals. The pedals change the pushing force of your leg muscles into a turning force. The chain uses the turning force to move a bike's back wheel.

## Let's Talk Torque

**Torque** is a turning force. Pushing a bike's pedals produces torque. Each pedal is at the end of a metal arm called a **crank**. The size of the torque is the force pushing the pedal multiplied by the length of the crank. Long cranks produce more torque than short cranks, making it easier to push the pedals around.

## Chain Reaction

Bicycles use a system called **chain drive**. A chain transfers power from the pedals to the wheel of the bike. Artist and inventor Leonardo da Vinci (1452–1519) first sketched a chain drive about 500 years ago. It was not until the 1880s, though, that it was used on a bike.

A bicycle's pedals turn a wheel called the **chainwheel**. A

Crank

Short crank = less torque

Crank

Long crank = more torque

◀ *If riders apply the same force to the pedals of these two bikes, the longer crank will produce more torque. If a crank were too long, however, the pedals would hit the ground!*

▲ *With a chain drive, a bike's pedals don't have to be fixed to the middle of the wheel. The driver doesn't have to sit on top of a huge front wheel, either! Chain-drive bicycles are a big improvement over the direct-drive penny-farthing.*

chainwheel is also called a **sprocket**. Teeth around the edge of the chainwheel fit into holes in the chain. Pushing the pedals turns the chainwheel, which pulls the chain around it. The chain turns another toothed wheel in the middle of the back wheel. That turns the rear wheel of the bike.

## Sit Up!

To push the pedals with the most force, a rider must sit in the correct position. If a bicycle seat is too low, the rider cannot push as hard. Raising the bike seat lets the rider pedal with more force. If the seat is too high, the rider's feet may not reach the ground!

# Swit hing Gea.

A bike is easy to ride on level ground, but pedaling uphill is hard work! Gears make it easier to pedal at a comfortable speed and with a comfortable force, no matter how steep the hill is.

## Force and Speed

When you ride a bike up a steep hill, you have to use a lot of force to move the pedals. You might stand up on the pedals and use your weight to help push them around. Gears let you change the force you must use. But there's a price to pay for easier pedaling. If you want to keep your speed the same, you have to pedal faster! It's a trade-off: Push the pedals hard and slowly, or change gear and pedal faster with less force.

## Get in Gear

A gearwheel is a toothed wheel. If two gearwheels the same size are connected by a bicycle chain, they turn at the same speed. If the gearwheels are different sizes, they turn at different speeds. A smaller gearwheel at the back

▲ *Riding uphill can be a struggle! By standing up, a rider uses body weight to help push the pedals.*

makes the rear wheel turn faster. A bigger gearwheel makes the rear wheel turn more slowly.

▲ *Different-size gearwheels turn the rear wheel at different speeds. Changing gear moves the chain from one gearwheel to another.*

# Gearing Up

How do you change gear? The chain must move from one gearwheel to another. Bicycles with gears have a set of gearwheels, all different sizes, in the middle of the back wheel. To change gear, the rider moves a lever. This makes the chain run off one gearwheel onto a smaller or bigger gearwheel next to it.

## Counting Teeth

Count the number of teeth on the chainwheel. Now count the number of teeth on the gearwheel in the middle of the bicycle's rear wheel. Divide the bigger number by the smaller number. The answer is a number called the **gear ratio**. It shows how many times the rear wheel turns for each turn of the pedals. If the gear ratio is 2, one turn of the pedals makes the rear wheel turn twice.

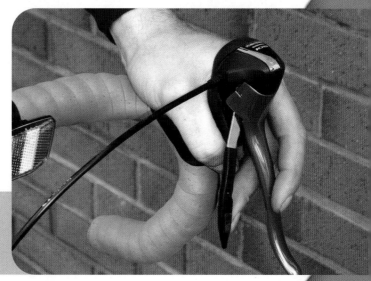

▶ *The bicycle rider moves a lever that pulls a cable to change gear.*

# Slow Down!

When you want to slow down a fast-moving bicycle, you need a large force acting against it. Friction works in the opposite direction to movement, so it can be used to slow or stop a bike. A bicycle's brakes work by making a lot of friction.

## Slow, Slower, Stop!

Most bikes have **caliper** brakes. A pad of tough material, such as hard rubber, is held on each side of a wheel. The brake pads do not touch the wheel unless the rider pulls a brake lever. Then the pads squeeze together and press against the wheel rim. There is a lot of friction between the brake pads and the wheel. Friction slows down the bicycle.

## Slip and Slide

Brakes that grip the rims of the wheels don't work well in rain or when a rider goes through puddles. If water gets between the brake pads and the wheel rim, there is less friction. The bike takes longer to stop. Bikes designed to go through mud and water sometimes have a different type of brake, called a **disc brake**. There is a disc at the

*▼ Pulling the brake lever tugs a cable, which squeezes the brake pads on the caliper against the wheel rim.*

Cable to brake lever

Caliper

Tire

Wheel rim

Brake pad          Brake pad

▲ *Brakes might not work well when they get wet. After riding through water, test your brakes.*

Another type of bike brake is called the **coaster brake**. It is in the center of the back wheel. A coaster brake works when the rider pedals backward.

center of each wheel. When the rider pulls the brake lever, a pair of tough pads squeeze together and grip the disc. This slows the wheel. When the bike goes through water, the disc stays drier than the wheel rims, because the disc is in the middle of the wheel.

## Skidding

If a rider brakes too hard, the wheels may suddenly stop turning while the bike is moving forward. That causes the wheels to skid. The rider has trouble controlling and balancing the bicycle.

# Energized to Action

You have to produce big forces to push a bike's pedals around, and you need **energy** to produce those forces. Energy and forces go together. There are different types of energy. When you ride a bike, energy changes from one type to another.

## The Sun's Energy

Where does energy come from? It all starts with the Sun. Sunlight gives plants energy to grow. People eat the plants. We also eat meat from animals that eat plants. We take in their energy and store it in our bodies. Then our muscles use the energy to produce the forces that do all sorts of things, such as pedaling a bicycle.

## Types of Energy

When something moves, it has a type of energy called **kinetic energy**. A moving bike, for example, has kinetic energy. The faster it moves, the more kinetic energy it has.

Riding uphill changes a bicycle's kinetic energy into a different kind of energy: **potential energy**. An object has potential energy because of its position. At the top

◀ *The energy you use when riding a bike comes from the food you eat. To keep fit and stay healthy, you need to eat a well-balanced diet.*

◀ When you ride a bike, your muscles change **chemical energy** from your food into kinetic energy.

## Lighting the Way

Some bicycle lights are powered by a **dynamo**. A dynamo is a small machine that changes kinetic energy into electrical energy. A little wheel on the dynamo presses against one of the bike wheels. When the bicycle wheel moves, it turns the dynamo wheel. The turning motion is changed into electricity that powers the bike's light.

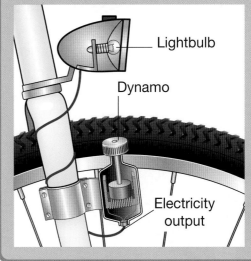

Lightbulb

Dynamo

Electricity output

of a hill, for example, a bike has a lot of potential energy. If you released the bike's brakes, the bike would start moving down the hill by itself. As the bike rolled downhill, its potential energy would change into kinetic energy.

## Vanishing Energy

Energy cannot be created or destroyed. It can only change from one type of energy to another. Scientists call this the **law of conservation of energy**.

Where does the energy go when a bike stops? When a rider uses a bike's brakes, friction between the wheels and the brakes heats them up. The kinetic energy changes into heat energy. If the brakes squeal, kinetic energy also changes into sound energy.

# Wheel Works

The center of a bicycle wheel is called the **hub**. It is joined to the rim by thin pieces of wire called **spokes**. Wheels with spokes are much lighter than solid metal wheels. Yet spoked wheels are very strong by design.

## Forces on Wheels

When a rider sits on a bike, the force of his or her weight tries to flatten the wheels. What stops the wheels from collapsing? Spokes help the wheels keep their circular shape. Half of the spokes go from the rim to one side of the hub. The other half of the spokes go from the rim to the other side of the hub. This gives the wheels extra strength and keeps them from bending or crumpling. Spokes make the wheels strong enough to withstand pedaling forces and braking forces, too.

## A Tense Situation

Bicycle spokes are usually made of thin steel wire. A spoke bends easily but is very hard to stretch or break by pulling at its ends. On a bicycle wheel, the spokes are tightened so that they pull the rim and hub toward each other with great force. This pulling, called **tension**, makes a spoked wheel stiff and strong.

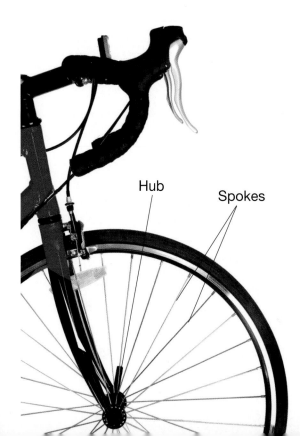

Hub

Spokes

◄ *A bicycle wheel with spokes is amazingly strong. It can support about 400 times its own weight!*

# Racing Wheels

Some racing bicycles have unusual wheels. The wheels may be solid, or they may have three or four wide, flat spokes.

Typical wire spokes stir up the air as a wheel turns, causing a lot of air resistance. That drag slows a bike down. A solid wheel or a wheel with fewer spokes cuts through the air more cleanly. It causes less drag. Wheels on racing bikes are often made from a lightweight material, such as carbon fiber.

▲ *BMX bikes have small, strong wheels with short spokes. The wheels are designed to withstand stunts and jumps without bending or breaking.*

▼ *Some racing bikes have solid wheels or wheels with wide, flat spokes. These wheels create less drag. They let racing cyclists go faster.*

# Rolling on Rubber

Bicycles have had rubber tires filled with air since John Boyd Dunlop invented them in 1888. Tires support the weight of the bike and the rider. They also carry the pedaling and braking forces to the ground.

## Pumped Up

When a rider sits on a bike, his or her weight squashes the tires at the bottom where they rest on the ground. The softer a tire is, the more the rider's weight squashes it. The flattening-out of the wheel causes **rolling resistance**. The rider must use more force to turn a wheel with a soft, squashy tire than a wheel with a hard tire. Why? More surface area is in contact with the road, so there is more friction—and less speed.

Most road bikes have thin tires pumped up to a high **pressure**. The high pressure makes the tires hard. Hard tires squash very little at the bottom, so the wheels have less rolling resistance. The cyclist can ride faster.

## Fat Tires

Mountain bikes are used on dirt and grass. Thin, hard tires don't work well on soft ground. That's why mountain bikes have fatter, softer tires that don't sink into the ground. Those tires have more rolling resistance, however. You won't see racers on mountain bikes in the Tour de France, the world's most famous road race!

▶ *A road bike's tires are pumped up to a high pressure. A bike with hard tires is easier to pedal than a bike with soft tires.*

24

# Tread Carefully

The part of a bicycle tire that touches the ground is called the **tread**. The tread is not smooth. A smooth tire would put the most rubber on the ground, creating the most grip, or friction. Smooth tires can't grip the ground well when the surface is wet, though. So the tread has grooves cut into it. The grooves move water out from under a tire so that the tread stays in contact with the ground.

*▲ Tires with a knobby tread grip soft, uneven ground well. The big bumps in the tread dig into the ground.*

*▶ The grooves in a bicycle tire squeeze water out from under the tire. That keeps the tire from skidding on a wet surface.*

## All Wet

When a bicycle goes through a puddle, water gets between the ground and a smooth tire. The tire actually floats on top of a thin film of water. If the tire doesn't touch the ground, there is no friction. The tire loses grip, resulting in **hydroplaning** (bottom).

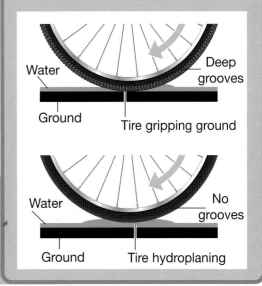

Water — Deep grooves

Ground — Tire gripping ground

Water — No grooves

Ground — Tire hydroplaning

# A Bumpy Ride

Some early bicycles were called boneshakers because their wooden wheels with iron tires rattled over bumps. All that shaking made the bikes hard to ride! Modern bikes are more comfortable to ride than the old-style bicycles of long ago.

## Springy Air

Modern bikes "soak up" or absorb bumps and jolts better than old-fashioned models did. Today, bicycles have rubber tires filled with air. Rubber is **flexible**. When a bike's wheel rolls over a small bump on the ground, the bump squashes the tire. The air inside the tire is squashed briefly, too. Then the tire springs back into shape.

## Springs and Things

Bicycles made for doing stunts or for riding on rough surfaces are designed to absorb bigger jolts. These bikes have springs that let the wheels move up and down when going over large bumps. A big spring, however, would keep bouncing up and down after passing over a bump. So the spring is coiled around another part, called a **damper**. This lets the spring squash fast but slows it down as it bounces back. Together, the two parts make up a **shock absorber**.

▼ *A bike with front suspension only is known as a hardtail.*

Front suspension

# Softening the Ride

A bicycle's springs and dampers are also called its **suspension** system. A bike might have no suspension, front suspension only, or both front and rear suspension. Front suspension is usually inside the front **fork**, the part that holds the bike's front wheel in position. It lets the front wheel move up and down. Rear suspension is usually provided by a shock absorber under the seat.

▼ *A bike with suspension at the front and back is said to have full suspension.*

Rear suspension

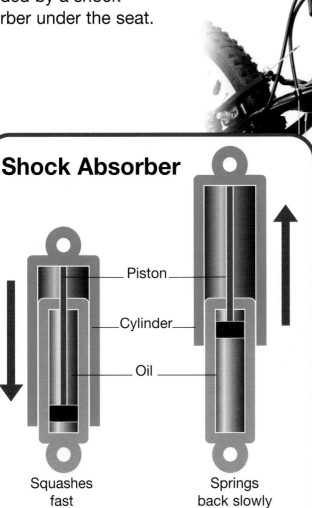

## Shock Absorber

Piston

Cylinder

Oil

Squashes fast

Springs back slowly

## Put a Damper on It

When a bike goes over a bump, its spring is squeezed together. The spring is attached to a damper. A damper is a tube full of oil, with a **piston** inside. The piston is pushed through the oil and forces the fluid through a small hole. That takes energy, which is changed into heat in the oil. The spring cannot spring back as quickly.

# Air Forces

The scientific study of objects moving through air is called **aerodynamics**. Aerodynamics is important in the design of cars and airplanes. It is important in the design of bicycles, too. Changing a bike's shape can let it speed through the air faster.

## What a Drag!

When you ride a bike, you push yourself and the bike through the air. The air pushes back, creating air resistance, or drag. Two types of drag affect bike riders. One is caused by pushing against the air in front of you. That is called **pressure drag**. As the air flows around you, it rubs against you.

This causes the second type of drag, called **skin friction**. Pressure drag slows you down more than skin friction does.

## A Need for Speed

Racing cyclists try to go as fast as possible. Their bikes are designed to reduce drag. The bike frames are made from oval or teardrop-shaped tubes instead of round tubes. Oval and teardrop-shaped tubes let air flow around them more easily. Wheels with spokes stir up the air and cause a lot of drag, so some racing bikes have solid wheels.

◀ *Low handlebars make a rider bend over lower. In this position, air flows smoothly over the rider's head and back, reducing drag.*

▲ *This racing cyclist wears a skintight suit and a specially shaped helmet to reduce skin friction.*

## Follow the Leader

Racing cyclists can keep riding fast without having to pedal as hard by doing something called **drafting**. A cyclist pushes against the air in front of him or her. That lowers the air pressure behind. When another cyclist rides close behind, the second cyclist rides inside the area of low-pressure air. That reduces the second cyclist's pressure drag, so he or she doesn't have to pedal as hard. Drafting lets the lead rider do the work of overcoming drag while the following rider uses less energy. If you watch a team of racing cyclists, you'll see a team member take the lead for a while as the other riders follow just inches behind.

▼ *In a race, cyclists ride very close together to reduce drag and save energy.*

# Glossary

**accelerate:** to change speed or direction

**aerodynamics:** the study of air acting on objects in motion

**air resistance:** a force that slows an object as it moves through air; also called *drag*

**caliper:** a device with two arms that can be squeezed together; used in bike brakes

**carbon fiber:** a very light, strong material made from thin strands of carbon in plastic

**center of gravity:** the point on an object at which gravity can be considered to act

**chain drive:** a way of transferring power from the pedals to the wheels of a bike

**chainwheel:** a wheel with teeth that fit into holes in a chain

**chemical energy:** stored energy, as in food, that changes form during chemical reactions

**coaster brake:** a brake that works by turning the pedals backward

**countersteering:** brief steering of a bicycle in the opposite direction at the beginning of a turn

**crank:** a part of a machine with a handle and a rod that turn and make the machine do work

**damper:** an oil-filled tube with a piston inside that absorbs energy to reduce the motion of a spring

**disc brake:** a type of brake with pads that are pressed against a disc at the center of a wheel

**drafting:** closely following in an area of low air pressure

**dynamo:** a machine that changes mechanical energy into electrical energy; sometimes used on a bicycle to power lights

**energy:** the ability to do work

**flexible:** easily bent or reshaped

**forces:** pulls or pushes that cause objects to move or change speed or direction of motion

**fork:** the part of a bike that holds the front wheel in position

**friction:** resistance to the sliding of objects against each other

**gear ratio:** the relationship between the number of teeth on gearwheels connected by a chain

**gearwheels:** toothed wheels

**gravity:** a force that pulls everything toward an object with mass, such as Earth

**gyroscopes:** spinning wheels that try to keep going in the same way

**hub:** the center part of a wheel

**hydroplaning:** skidding when a film of water on a surface makes tires lose contact with it

**kinetic energy:** energy of motion

**law of conservation of energy:** a scientific rule that states that energy cannot be created or destroyed but can change form

**laws of motion:** scientific laws that state relationships between the forces acting on an object and the motion of the object

**piston:** a sliding piece moved against fluid pressure

**potential energy:** stored energy

**pressure:** pressing or squeezing

**pressure drag:** the resistance of air in front of a moving object

**recumbent:** lying down

**rolling resistance:** a force that tries to stop a wheel from moving

**shock absorber:** a device that lessens jolts to give a smooth ride

**skin friction:** resistance caused by contact of air against the surface of an object

**spokes:** thin bars that connect the hub of a wheel to the rim

**sprocket:** a chainwheel

**suspension:** the springs and shock absorbers that give a smooth ride on bumpy ground

**teeth:** parts that stick out on a wheel

**tension:** the condition of being stretched tight, with no slack

**torque:** a turning or twisting force

**tread:** the part of a tire that touches the ground

**weight:** the heaviness of an object, caused by gravity pulling it toward the center of Earth

# Find Out More

**The Exploratorium's Science of Cycling**
*www.exploratorium.edu/cycling*
Information about bicycle science

**How Stuff Works: How Bicycles Work**
*www.howstuffworks.com/ bicycle.htm*
The basics of how bikes work

**Publisher's note to educators and parents:** Our editors have carefully reviewed these web sites to ensure that they are suitable for children. Many web sites change frequently, however, and we cannot guarantee that a site's future contents will continue to meet our high standards of quality and educational value. Be advised that children should be closely supervised whenever they access the Internet.

# Index